Permanent Address

Poems by

Lorna Knowles Blake

The Ashland Poetry Press
Ashland University
Ashland, Ohio 44805

Printed in the United States of America

ISBN: 978–0-912592–61–9

Library of Congress Catalog Card Number: 2007933909

Book cover photo by Chris Windsor, Getty Images

Cover graphic design by Mike Ruhe

Author photo by James J. Kriegsman

How Much Home Does a Person Need? Jean Améry, Sidney Rosenfeld and Stella P. Rosenfeld, translators, reprinted from *At the Mind's Limits*, p. 41, © 1980, Indiana University Press: Bloomington and Indianapolis, Indiana.

"Are You?" copyright © 2004 by Dorothea Tanning, reprinted from *A Table of Content: Poems*, published by Graywolf Press: Saint Paul, Minnesota.

The author wishes to express her grateful acknowledgment to the editors of the following publications, in which these poems, some in earlier versions, first appeared.

Barrow Street, "Darwin's Doxology"
Bellingham Review, "Permanent Address," "Rondeau" and "Sundowning"
BigCityLit, "Desert Island Disc" and "Exogamy"
Calyx, "Because I have no accent" and "Revolution Box"
The Connecticut Review, "December Dilemmas"
Crab Orchard Review, "Dulce de Leche" and "King Sugar"
Dogwood, "Carnation, Lily, Lily, Rose"
The Formalist, the first sonnet of "Conversion," "Hallel" and "Miniature"
The Hudson Review, "Book of Hours," "Bedtime Story," "Proverbs of Hell" and "Washashores"
Iambs and Trochees, "Rats in the Sacristy"
Lumina, "Autumn Argument," "Body of Water," "Notions" and "Shabbat, Riverside Park"
Mars Hill Review, "Quotidian"
Pivot, "An Evening Prayer"
Rattapallax, "Eden," "Luncheon of the Boating Party" and "Wish Fulfillment"
Sewanee Theological Review, "Prothalamion"
Tar River Poetry, "Migraine"

The poems "After a Fight," "American Girl®," "Little Spanish Lessons," "On Quivett Creek," "Saved Letters," "Seasonal Aubade," "The Art of Translation," "To a Teenage Daughter" and "Winter, Rock Harbor" appeared in the feature *Twelve* in the Spring 2008 issue of *BigCityLit*.

The poem "My Memoir" appeared in the anthology *Ravishing DisUnities: Real Ghazals in English* (Wesleyan University Press, 2000). "Conversion" appeared in *Sonnets: 150 Contemporary Sonnets* (University of Evansville Press, 2005). "Harbor Watch" appeared in *Chance of a Ghost* (Helicon Nine Editions, 2005).

"Eden" was nominated for a Pushcart Prize. "Transitional Objects" was published in the 2005 New England Poetry Contest anthology. "Rainy Day: Paris" won an honorable mention in the Morton Marr Poetry Contest of the *Southwest Review*. "King Sugar," "Miniature" and "Notions" also appeared on *Verse Daily*.

"Miniature" is dedicated to the memory of Adie Mitchell.

Special thanks to Anne Hopkins Campbell, Michelle Friedman and Rachel Wetzsteon for igniting the spark; to Martin Mitchell for innumerable kindnesses; to Greg Nicholl for his help and advice; to all my family and friends for their patience and love; to Rachel Hadas, Charles Martin, Vijay Seshadri and all the writers and teachers at the Johns Hopkins Summer Seminar, Sarah Lawrence College, the Sewanee Writers' Conference, the West Chester Poetry Conference and the 92nd Street Y for their support, inspiration and encouragement. Grateful acknowledgment is also due the Virginia Center for the Creative Arts for providing the time and space for writing and revising this work.

for my husband and daughter
and
in memory of my parents

Contents

I

Because I have no accent/3
Wish Fulfillment/5
Carnation, Lily, Lily, Rose/6
An Evening Prayer/7
Prothalamion/8
Notions/9
Exogamy/10
At Shiloh/11
Hallel/12
Rondeau/13
Luncheon of the Boating Party/14
Rainy Day: Paris/15
After a Fight/16
Washashores/17
Autumn Argument/19

II

Revolution Box/23
King Sugar/24
Dulce de Leche/26
On Quivett Creek/27
Desert Island Disc/28
Harbor Watch/29
Winter, Rock Harbor/30
December Dilemmas/31
Seasonal Aubade/33
Shabbat, Riverside Park/34
Body of Water/35
To a Teenage Daughter/36
American Girl®/38
Miniature/39
Permanent Address/40

III

Eden/43
Darwin's Doxology/44
Rats in the Sacristy/45
Conversion/46
Transitional Objects/48
Sundowning/49
Bedtime Story/50
Quotidian/51
Migraine/52
Saved Letters/54
My Memoir/55
Proverbs of Hell/57
A Book of Hours/62
Little Spanish Lessons/65
The Art of Translation/66

Notes/67

I

How much home does a person need?
—Jean Améry

Because I have no accent

people always ask me,
In what language do you dream?
By the ocean, always in Spanish—

Naranja dulce, limón partido—
my sisters are turning a rope,
calling out their counting rhymes

in the shade of an old *roble*,
which is an elm tree if I dream
I'm somewhere else. In the distance

islands bead the horizon
into a chain of names: *Isla Culebra,*
Isla Mona, Caja de Muertos. Seconds later

the scene turns cool; mossy
green hills rise from low stone
walls as the island becomes Ireland.

Now the boot of English
steps on my dream's slender neck,
until Great-grandmother's murmuring

Celtic diphthongs fill my sleep,
rustling like sails that propel me
into her safe harbor of softer vowels.

Sleinte, she calls, as I return
to the crisp cadences of parents
and their houseguests, who mingle,

consonants clinking like ice cubes
in highballs brought out to the pool.
Two *criadas* cut up *guanábanas* and gossip

while the children of the house
lurk in the kitchen, listening to wild
romances on the *radio-novela*. Voices fade,

my dream stalls in the city's
glottal morning, but all night long
I travel over language, that swaying bridge.

Wish Fulfillment

In a spring of hope and mistrust, planting vines and petunias
to attract hummingbirds—

their passion for red, shimmer and flash, swill of nectar,
the dart and hover of wings—

I doubted the power of vines, doubted the power of anything,
to attract. No birds came,

though a plague of aphids beset the hibiscus. Up in the locust tree,
two crows clamored at sunrise

and a phoebe repeated her sweet two-note song. I learned to love
the world for all it doesn't grant,

but my dreams sparkled: *sapphire-crested, emerald-bellied, ruby-throated,
amethyst-crowned, rufous-breasted.*

Summer slouched on and on, and one day a hummingbird stalled
in the amazed morning air—hover and dart—

then vanished, swift as the instant just before waking, when
you get what you always wanted.

Carnation, Lily, Lily, Rose
John Singer Sargent

Here, there is no before and no after,
only a summer evening in the garden,
the perfect disappearing now of dusk
caught, as in a jar, held for a moment.

It's a summer evening in a garden
of cascading color: carmine, green and gold
caught in a jar and held for a moment.
Twilight brightened by Japanese lanterns,

and cascades of color—carmine, green and gold—
all contained in a vanishing instant.
Twilight, brightened by Japanese lanterns
aglow in clouds of lilies engulfed by roses,

is contained in a vanishing instant
it took the painter two years to record.
Under clouds of lilies engulfed by roses,
faces solemn with the concentration

it took the painter two years to record,
stand two young sisters in white pinafores.
Their faces solemn with concentration,
kindling lamps that turn flowers to stars,

two young sisters in white pinafores
prolong evening, push the darkness away.
Kindling lamps that turn flowers to stars,
he must have struck thousands of matches

to prolong evening, to push darkness away
from here, where there is no before or after.
He must have struck thousands of matches
to paint this perfect disappearing now.

An Evening Prayer

Oh, deliver me from the familiar,
from the old maps and their destinations
that are pre-destinations, nothing more.
Ransom me from the phone call at dinner,
the clock's impudent digital flip at midnight,
the car alarm, insistent urban rooster, at dawn.
Quiet the ululations of the wind, comfort
the mourning dove in her unstoppable grief,
lighten the night's weary reprisal of events,
silence the oracle's tedious midlife whine,
prophecies the self fulfills again and again.

Grant me a drink from the cool blue stream
of dreamless sleep. Redeem me from broken
promises, from petty tyrannies of remorse.
Draw me out from the still waters of exile,
lead me away from the unchanging thicket
of the past, walk me through the hedges
of all previous attempts, into a garden
where spent flowers curl into fat buds,
dry leaves float up from the ground, furling
into tight green cocoons of possibility,
and colorful songbirds, startled, are blown
backward into the bright, unruly present.

Prothalamion

Marriage begins in the giving of words.
—Wendell Berry

Love will pitch a tent anywhere—
at the edge of a cliff in a hurricane wind,
on a great ocean of grass
just as the tornado approaches—
and whisper reckless promises
of permanence, sincerely meant.

Marriage vows to build a home:
walls and rooms to move between,
an attic, stairs, a few hiding places,
doors, an open window, shuttered
sometimes; now add lamps, mirrors,
a drawer that locks, a bookcase wide

enough to shelve the crowded past,
the stories yet to come. Set the cornerstone
on this wedding day—Love always
insists, *it will blow over us,* but storms
will come and in a house of words
you stand a chance, a fighting chance.

Notions

Just like Eve in the garden,
who knew the word *fruit*
but not its implications, a bride
wanders through store aisles.

She sees buttons, grommets,
pinking shears, needles, spools
of mercerized thread, and doesn't
think *fastened, trimmed, mended.*

Sees bolts of fabric, doesn't think
bias, cut. When the apple-shaped
pincushion catches her eye,
she doesn't yet think *heart, pierced.*

Exogamy

When love arrives and spreads its naïve gloss
thick as almond icing on a wedding cake,
we've only gained a mate and nothing's lost.

We're counting blessings, not amortizing costs,
at least not yet; as newlyweds who make
a home with the Mezuzah and the Cross,

we boldly plan to forge our way across
the complications. We have what it takes—
love conquers all and the world's well lost.

On holidays, the in-laws we have tossed
together try to conceal their heartbreak;
cloaked in advice, their words sound cross,

until a granddaughter arrives, embossed
with double dreams and histories that ache.
We start on life's long calculus of loss

as sacrifices settle like April frost
on tender shoots. Not even for our sake
can true love wring a gain from every loss
ushered in by the Mezuzah and the Cross.

At Shiloh

And Hannah prayed, for she was in bitterness of soul.
                                    I Samuel 1:10

I can find no consolation here—
only heat-stricken olive trees,

the cramping grief of another month,
and Peninnah, belly yeasting

with child again. I fold myself
into silence, licking my ache, sucking

my sorrow like a bone. I cannot eat; I am fat
with longing, fat with my portion

of meat and desolation.
"Hannah, why do you weep? Why do you not eat?

Why are you sad? Am I not more to you than ten sons?"
I hate his blind love.

Each time he knows me,
I lie on my pillows while the crickets sing,

imagine a child's damp weight in my arms,
the rise and fall of his breath.

The burnt offering sickens me,
the flaying chatter ... how hot it is. How hot!

There is nothing left to do—

Hallel

My daughter sings the ancient prayers, she brings
home melodies sung by the children's choir
like arts and crafts. Among her treasured things,
      my daughter sings.

Her words are strangers, but I never tire
of them. I welcome the chants and blessings
she ushers in; her newfound friends inspire

me, even after she has flown on wings
of sleep—an echo of the shepherd's lyre,
the psalmist's praise, the cantor's tenor rings—
      my daughter sings.

Rondeau

I followed her for miles: along Broadway,
across to Central Park, happy to delay
my weekend obligations, taking time
to enjoy this bright surprise, so sublime
amid the caps and hats (that Saturday

morning I had heard the weatherman say
that temperatures were in the nineties—way
above normal for June and expected to climb).
I followed her for miles

(the paper reports that Swiss workers lay
yards of insulation over the Alps in May
to keep the glaciers cool in summertime),
until she vanished near the Guggenheim,
her yellow parasol no longer on display.
                    I'd followed her for miles.

Luncheon of the Boating Party
Pierre-Auguste Renoir

The oarsman's arms are beautiful,
set off by sleeveless white cotton.
He straddles the chair, leaning back
as oarsmen do, confident that mere space
wouldn't dare let him fall. His profile,
under the black band of his straw boater
(So *that* is why they call it a boater!),
suggests a handsome geniality so
seductive one longs for an introduction
to the man himself. Gustave Caillebotte,
the catalogue informs, wealthy patron,
close friend and fellow Impressionist,
posed with his back to the viewer,
enjoying a postprandial cigarette
on a shaded riverside balcony crowded
with company: actresses, artists, models
and *flaneurs*. Alphonsine, the proprietor's
pretty daughter, leans against the railing,
admiring his well-defined physique
and the sleek satisfaction he sheds
like water. She has an enviable spot:
a perfectly unobstructed view—

I would step into that empty space
to his left (with a sidelong glance
from under my most fetching hat,
the lacy trim on my sleeve accidentally
brushing his biceps) and whisper secrets
I know about love and immortality:
that his most famous painting
will be unveiled over and over again,
unfurling impressions of rainy beauty
each time an umbrella, purchased
in the museum gift shop, opens.

Rainy Day: Paris
inspired by Gustave Caillebotte

March is not the prettiest month to visit—
damp and chilly—still, there are times the painter
needs a subtle yellow to glaze the cloudy
        scene on his easel.

Noisy students dawdle and housewives linger
on the sidewalk chatting, their voices swooping
down like sparrows gathered in stolen hours of
        coveted sunlight.

Those in suits and satchels avoid the metro,
cutting through the greening parks, taking breakfast
pour emporter, strolling and nibbling pastries,
        pausing at windows.

When the rain begins, there's a scramble; people
huddle under awnings until umbrellas
open, turning bridges and boulevards to
        meadows of asphalt,

swirling fields of waterproof plaids and florals.
No one minds the weather's confusion or the
windy dodge and fluster because it's spring, it's
        only a lover's

quarrel with the world; and we're like familiar
painted figures crossing the sluicing, cobbled
streets, composed beneath skies of stormy canvas,
        caught in the downpour.

After a Fight

there is the cold, dark sea
of separation to row across
with one oar,

and I am already exhausted,
desperate to drift and drift and drift
on a current of sleep...

I must make my way back,
and touch you lightly
so you will turn toward me
before the world bears down again.

Washashores

Saint's Landing, Brewster, Massachusetts

September, and the garden's blown
    and bolted, wren and finch have flown
south, and the sun sets farther down

the bay each passing night. We hate
    the thought of leaving; contemplate
alternatives, as if this bright

and ample season could endure
    beyond the calendar's secure
curfew, but Labor Day is here

and autumn is ready to sue
    for possession. What do we do?
Procrastinate, then pack and go—

my books, your music, linen clothes
    and one more summer is foreclosed
upon by rituals such as these:

stacking canoes and wicker chairs,
    arguing over small repairs
required by weather or the years.

Where is the pulse of a home? What
    is the soul of a house? That
marriage of dwelling and spirit?

Perhaps it's in the flow of tide,
    a herring gull's suspended glide,
the constant birdsong in the shade

reminding us: you are, you are.
    Then, just before we load the car,
the house fills with the airy fire

of sunset and we shroud the place
  in bedding, a green-sprigged embrace
of percale and flannel and fleece.

Is it love, I wonder, when we're done
  or time we're shielding from the sun,
beneath these sheets that we slept on?

Autumn Argument

You would wake each day of the year
in leaf season, a permanent
blaze of foliage resistant
to gravity, rainstorm, wind shear.

Not for you the promiscuous
fields of summer—endless green, green,
green; nor spring waiting unseen
in the mud, full of amorous

rebirth; and not the ashen pall
of winter. Yes, you'd freeze your grove
in flames, but I tell you—we love
the autumn leaves because they fall.

II

All homes are home; mirages everywhere.
—Dorothea Tanning

Revolution Box

On the short-wave radio Fidél droned on and on,
though she never appeared to listen—after all,
there had been so many revolutions. Once shots
were fired at the house; the mirror on the wall
shattered, but no one was hurt.
                              Havana was home,
yet she kept a metal box in the entry hall
closet, filled with family photographs, passports,
her mother's *Book of Common Prayer*, small
tins of condensed milk and two hand-embroidered
tablecloths. To her grandchild, it was magical,
this readiness for going, the preparedness for flight.
If I wondered where we would go, I can't recall
asking, bred as we were for sudden emigration.
I liked to look at the pictures, liked the little
replenishments; the domestic attention given
to the box seemed comforting, traditional
as Christmas baking, spring cleaning or her summer
tea party.
              And every year the white and green tiled
kitchen was stocked with bags of sugar, canning jars,
pounds of oranges in red mesh bags. A special
tool peeled the pebbled skin into continuous strips,
large enameled kettles of water came to a boil,
and the house filled with the scent of citrus cooking
down to marmalade. Fidél's voice sounded tall
and firm but indistinct, like distant marching feet.
Outside, the tamarind and mango trees let fall
their ripe and unused fruit. Inside, she kept busy:
she went on canning oranges imported from Seville,
as if we might starve in all that tropical abundance.

King Sugar

Sugarcane harvest:
an arc of machetes
scythes down,
decapitated stalks
fall like soldiers crossed
on the fields. A smell
rises in the heat, so sweet
the air itself sickens.

The *cañaveral* is full
of spiders and armies
of men in straw hats,
shaded faces, backs
burnished to mahogany,
advancing like a wave
in an unbroken rhythm
over a land of cane.

Trundling carts carry
loads of oozing stalks
to be refined into sugar
and fire ripples over
the stubble of roots,
incinerating the land,
leaving a wake of black
remnants glowing
in the cremated fields.

Clouds of black ash
drift over the town.
We dust and clean;
black snow keeps falling.
Dust and clean and dust.
"It's positively biblical,"
you say, "the burning fields,
ash falling like a plague"

... or a sign that we all
burn for a pure white
sweetness at the core.

Dulce de Leche

Ahead of us a man asks for his coffee
extra light, fuel against the winter night.

The frozen food case is heating up—lime
sorbet, mango madness, passion fruit glacé.

In the fogged glass my mother blooms
briefly, wearing a flowered shirtwaist dress

in a tiled kitchen slick with island heat,
late morning moistened by the steam

rising from pots filled with boiling cans
of condensed milk—she must be making

the caramel paste we loved to spread
on toast, slices of fruit, our fingers.

And tonight in a Broadway deli, rows
of crystal-crusted lids announce a new

exotic flavor of premium ice cream—
Dulce de Leche sighs the Scandinavian label

on the pint we carry home. "What does it mean?"
my daughter asks. "Sweetness of milk or...

milk candy," I tell her as the words melt
on my tongue like memories, lost in translation.

On Quivett Creek

We were not quite lost that Sunday
morning: two hours of high tide left

as the water began its alchemy from salt
to mineral, luring us into bosky silence—

small choirs in the pine trees, a breeze
ruffling the cordgrass, waves slapping

against the shore. Each turn compelled us
farther, we let ourselves go with the water,

forward; without charts, the looping ribbon
of creek became both route and destination.

Houses tucked into the marsh drowsed
behind drawn shades, indifferent to us,

shorebirds ignored us, busy with their own
tasks and hungers, and past the last bend,

or the next-to-last, past the osprey nesting
station, just before the cemetery, bells rang.

And if you were to die today, or leave me,
if memory is all we ever have of eternity,

this is the moment I'd choose to remember—
a green hereafter of sunlight and pealing bells.

Paddles raised, kayaks slowly pirouetting
in the sun, we floated, listening long after

the last echo's faint splash, until the tide
carried us on its backward journey to the bay.

Desert Island Disc

Kind of Blue. *It's my desert island disc.*
—Overheard in a bar

Could anything be lonelier than this?
Scenario: you're on a desert island,
surrounded by blue ocean, air and mist.
Could anything be lonelier than this
scenario? You wonder if you're even missed
by anyone, or if you could have planned
a situation lonelier than this
scenario. You're on a desert island,

but not alone beneath brushed satin skies;
though you may be all blue, or kind of blue.
You have your music, and it never lies
or leaves you lonely. Under satin skies
a trumpet plays from sunset to sunrise—
the air itself turns *Blue in Green* in blue.
You'd never be alone beneath those skies,
though you might be *All Blue* or *Kind of Blue.*

Harbor Watch

I think of you, Mary Alice, in your small house by the sea,
telescope trained on the harbor, shipping news on the desk,

your small snort of satisfaction as boats sortie and return
on schedule. Your house feels cozy, haphazard, overstuffed

with antique furniture more suited to an earlier, grander home.
Rows of gilt-framed ancestors line the walls, our people's wild

slash of eyebrows watching you, intent on ships anchored
in the harbor of your telescope, a strange, three-legged bird

more alive than all that mahogany. You wake to the reliable
comforts of a light's rhythmic sweep, a foghorn's steady

basso profundo, your own voice fading like chintz and memories.
Small lapses surprise you into confusion: was it L—or H—

who married before the war, or was it after? Was it in town,
or on the beach at Sandy Cove? Details disintegrate like motes

in sunlight. Mary Alice, the ship you wait for won't be listed
in those pages. It will glide, dreamlike, into the glass eye

of that waiting telescope, your ghosts all gathered on the deck,
so many pale hands like white scarves, waving, beckoning.

Winter, Rock Harbor

Mile-long, a gleaming white slag of glacial sea,

salt-ice, the beach today an expanse more like

    snowcap or permafrost—seductive,

though I'm aware of the danger: floes will

break up, despite their solid appearance. Still,

life churns beneath in currents that only seem

    landlocked—a trick of winter ocean

weather. *Now come*, it calls, *walk on water*,

change elements. A January blizzard has

freeze-framed the two of us on this spectral bay—

    wild, cold and glorious—tidal flats we

rambled for miles all those careless summers.

December Dilemmas

In this version of the O. Henry story
he doesn't pawn his gold pocket watch,
she doesn't sell her hair to buy presents
sweet with irony. Instead, she lights
double the number of candles
she used to, and he buys her a tree.

She is grateful for the Christmas tree
but the crèche, so crucial to the story,
is missing, and she misses the candles
on the advent wreath. They both watch
the carolers sing, haloed by streetlights;
at home, she keeps busy wrapping presents.

He worries that so many presents
piled up under the star-topped tree
trimmed in red glass and white lights
is a betrayal of his people's history:
the Maccabees' eight-night watch
repeated each year with eight candles.

If only it were as simple as candles
on a frosted cake and birthday presents
everyone agrees on: doll, bicycle, watch.
Now they have a child who loves the tree
but is utterly confused by the stories,
which do seem to be mostly about lights

to help pass the dark midwinter. Lights
on houses, windows lamp-lit with candles
illuminate this or that made-up story
from a wondrous past that presents
a mishmash of traditions: pagan trees,
gifts of the magi, the shepherds' watch.

And this family keeps its double watch
of solstice festivals with all the lights
ablaze on his menorah and her tree,
hoping that the bright heat of the candles
and the excitement of opening presents
will make up for the loss of their stories.

But watch: their child will create a new story
of seasonal delight; the Tree is just a tree,
and candles only mean eight nights of presents.

Seasonal Aubade

Late last night we turned on daylight
saving. Lucky hour's wild spree,
springing forward, falling back, free
little bird enraptured by flight—

as who would not be, to escape
the ticking tyranny of clocks
and time's rough shocks and aftershocks?
Midnight assumes its usual shape:

in bed, you watch the slow hands creep
toward morning, toss and turn, while
a dream I'm dreaming makes me smile.
At dawn, you're wrestled into sleep

just when I'm leaving for the park
to walk the dog. The room is warm,
your body shifts, I touch your arm
goodbye and day breaks in the dark.

Shabbat, Riverside Park

In the slow time of a Saturday
in June, on the promenade,
under an alley of sycamores,
their Cezanne-like bark smooth
bone-yellow and peeling gray,
neighbors are at rest and play.

They seem chosen for chromatic
value to the composition: dark
man, silver bike, blond child,
brown dog. The scene is so lovely
it merits an elegant French title
on a brass plaque at the museum.

You and I are in the picture too,
on a park bench; commanded
by our faith to repose, it seems
we are caught in a bright green
net—as if we were only filters
for color and light, and life

were not a passing calendar
full of encounters and evasions;
as if all the trouble and violence
of our shattered world were not
waiting: feral, crouched,
in the pages of the Sunday papers.

Body of Water

She dives into the dark dissolving blue,
down deep, where light is just a wavy sheen
on the surface and lungs begin to pine
for air; floats up until the undertow
wraps her wrist in kelp and tugs her under.
Just where borders vanish between the sea
and sky, she breaks free, strokes across the bay
as far as she can go, and then surrenders.

Awash in blue above and blue below,
she doesn't see the clouds or hear the thunder,
ignores the waving arms and calls from shore:
not here, she thinks, there is no danger here.
The rain on her salt-stung face feels tender,
lovely—but she turns and swims back to you.

To a Teenage Daughter

If I'd had access to a crystal ball,
I might have timed things differently, and all
this strife would morph into a fantasy
as plausible as one of those TV
sitcoms you watch every night; shows that sell
you body products you don't need and tell
fairy tales in pixels. Mothers have fled,
gone mad or are conveniently dead,
and daughters pace a clear hormonal field.
No one, Menarche, would be left to yield
to the drawn arrow of your quivering youth,
you could scorch all the worn maternal earth
your teenaged moon-fed bloodlust hungers for
and I'd be a fond memory, nothing more.

But as it happens, Love, I'm here in blood
and flesh, and plain as air or the wet mud
that sucks red shoes into the swamp of life;
stuck in your slender side, I am the knife
that pierces your heart's independent dreams.
My glorious opponent, it may seem
our battle lines are drawn, but Menopause,
fat, almost fifty and riddled with flaws,
is frightened by rebellious Menarche,
whose only crime is that she lives to be.
Still, Menopause is dangerous; although
a gibbous, waning moon propels her through
these wars, cunning corrects those deficits.
The young move in starts, the older in fits.

So, Daughter, let us walk across this swoon,
this crazy field of love and blood and moon;
I will retreat and pass on the baton,
assuming elder status on life's throne,
accept your change of terms and walk away
from a role I'd naïvely planned to play,

starring in your life a few more seasons;
but life is ruled by nature, not by reason.
Your favorite show is now "The Gilmore Girls":
a very young mother and daughter swirled
like marble cake, occasionally crazed,
seductive, sweetly intimate in ways
contrived by focus groups, not life, not years,
certainly not hormones or these tears.

American Girl®

Let's be friends, whisper the beautiful dolls,
their cheeks tinted pink, their lips tinted rose,
complete with masses of thick, shiny hair,
        eyes that open and close
and named Samantha, or Molly, or Rose.

Each doll arrives with a six-chapter book—
inspiring tales of pluck and adventure.
These stories are the heart of the affair,
        claims the glossy brochure,
but collecting is the real adventure

in this catalogue of seductions: page
after page of old-fashioned toys, dresses
for the dolls, furniture, accessories,
        brushes for their tresses
and life-sized copies of those dresses

for little girls delirious with desire.
They can't resist the outfits and well-made
miniature props that go with each story:
        tea cakes and lemonade,
wicker chairs far lovelier than home-made

alternatives. And that's what this clever
company counts on—the innocent greed
of girls and a passion for collection
        that spreads like garden weeds:
how seamlessly our wants become our needs!

Miniature

The dollhouse builder loves to be in charge;
a master of proportion, he's aware
that little rooms make children's hands feel large

enough to make decisions—who sleeps where,
or place a porcelain bathtub in the hall,
and prop the baby in a grownup's chair.

He traces flowers on a papered wall
and smooths the flaxen hair from a doll's face,
wondering, as he does, if a thing so small

can't help but feel a passive kind of grace
as hands move her from place to place to place.

Permanent Address

Two blank lines for the
application form's
    unsettling question.

In my leather book
streets and postal codes
    faded or crossed out,

stamped cards and letters
sent wherever home
    was at the time; now

these are the houses
of photographs and
    dreams, where I still see

a girl's room, a swing,
a crape myrtle tree.
Always sedulous,

memory goes on
charting its atlas
    of imaginary

places—some radiant,
some ruined—in mind.
A Baedeker for

natives of nowhere,
travelers from birth.
    Our one sure address?

Circle and star on
a billboard map that
    shows us: *you are here.*

III

*Birds in flight, claims the architect
Vincenzo Volentieri, are not between
places; they carry their places with them.
We never wonder where they live: they
are at home in the sky, in flight. Flight is
their way of being in the world.*
—Geoff Dyer

Eden

In a perfect world spinning adjacent
to this one, I name the animals,
divide day from night, etc. Enthralled,
I pronounce it good and then, complacent,
I rest, in firm control of my nascent
universe. *Don't wake me up.* Why must all
creation be vexed by longing? I fall

again and again into desires sent
nightly to trouble my dreams, demanding
their own worlds, forests, mythical beasts
to tame. Yet over there, the rain has always
just ended, the garden keeps expanding
its boundaries, time's drip-drip has ceased
and fruit waits to be plucked. I may, someday...

Darwin's Doxology

Praise that roseate spoonbill,
this rose-breasted grosbeak,
every finch and every flower;
praise vegetable and mineral,
carnivore and herbivore, snake
and quadruped; praise creatures
apterous, edentate, mammalian,
crustacean, mono-valved and bi-;
praise those with gills and fins
and lungs: all that are here,
observed and classified, the fleet,
the shy, the predatory and the sly.
Praise variations yet to come,
and those preserved in stone;
praise the fire in the bone.

Praise, praise, praise:
let it rain, let it pour, let it flow...

Rats in the Sacristy

Even before I genuflect, it starts.
I hear them when the collect of the day
begins, "Almighty God, to whom all hearts
are open, all desires known," I pray

but they are gnawing at my confidence.
Though choir and hymns will try to drown them out,
descant and organ closing like a fence
around my faith can't shield me from the doubt.

Their scrabbling chitter is the antiphon
of every chanted psalm. I keep my mind
focused on brilliant pools of stained glass sun,
the haloed heads of children ... still I find

no sanctuary from them—even here—
these insolent, smart creatures that I fear.

Conversion
after Georges de la Tour

A nocturne deep in shadows seems to frame
the pensive Magdalen as she sits alone,
her glinting jewels darken to common stone,
her fine clothes weave a red brocade of shame.
She contemplates the image of the flame
in the mirror, a taller chaperone
to the candle's graceful plume of light, shown
twice, as if meant to enlighten and inflame.

Conversion by candlelight: Mary's hands
rest on a skull in her lap, its ocher stain
the color of regret—to watch her choose
between mirror and candle, the demands
of self and truth, evokes a kindred pain
in anyone who has a past to lose.

~

A yellow flame now blazes to command
her gaze, curling into a smoky filament,
a visible sigh; its incandescent
light bathes a stark tableau of books, cross and
a length of knotted rope, a scourge to brand
on flesh the welcome sting of punishment.
Pain's sweet distraction makes a sacrament
of guilt all penitents can understand.

A tenebrae of lamplight, blood and bone:
the trilling cascade of cream-colored sleeve,
one shoulder bare, her crossed feet also bare,
subdued by shadows, ready to atone,
she recollects the day she was reprieved,
and washed his feet in tears and flowing hair.

~

The dreamy gaze, intense and yet serene,
the parted lips, loose hair and dishabille
suggest a lover's sorrowful appeal—
there's more to this repentant Magdalene,
whose warm breath bends the dying flame between
the book and mirror. Secrets long concealed
in corners yield to candles and she yields,
heart-struck, to the man who made her clean.

Love will always seek to change its object;
a source of light, so numinous and pure,
redeems the warm penumbra of the paint
with a golden glow, until its subject
becomes, in this mystery of *claire-obscure,*
a radiant conflation: woman, legend, saint.

Transitional Objects

Are we not strange creatures that we go and place
our affections from earliest years where they remain hopeless?
—Rainer Maria Rilke

Before the last of nineteen moves across
cities, countries, continents—and recently
widowed—she began sending out boxes

of things: a '69 yearbook sent to the child
who graduated in '72; emerald earrings
intended for a daughter's May birthday

appeared in October, greening autumn's
fiery iridescence. The family historian
waited months for letters she had mailed

to his incurious brother, a jazz musician
mourning a pile of scratched 78s carted
off by her janitor's boy. I'm the lucky one—

my package delivers three worn dolls.
I lay them out, stroke their hair, smooth
their gauzy, wrinkled gowns and wonder

why my dolls were spared: silent tutors
of the nursery, impassive victims
of violent tantrums and extravagant love.

She must have loved them, too—I think
of my daughter's smelly, threadbare dog—
loyal conscript, confederate, confidante.

Is this the toy's dark gift? To let us
lavish ourselves on a plastic cheek, a head
of frazzled curls, a faded matt of plush.

Sundowning

No celestial bodies herald
   night, no sun sinks below
the horizon; here time

is measured by heartbeat,
   heartbeat, heartbeat:
a machine's urgent chimes.

The tableau in our room
   recomposes to hear news;
semblance of the calendar

intrudes: day six, they say,
   or in the next twelve hours...
Is this Monday's crossword?

Yesterday's flat soda? A latte
   from the daily coffee run
rests on the windowsill; friends

congregate in waiting rooms,
   recall times shared—
the past the only outcome

we can trust. They leave us
   to the lulling whoosh and blip
of your departure, but our vigil

fails; we need to sleep, and eat;
   you slip away as time
fails us again. You'll be gone

when we return, each of us
   carrying our story
of a you that is, and is not, you.

Bedtime Story

On your night table I found
the novel you'd begun to read
two weeks before you died,
turned down at page fifty-five.
The ten last days you were alive
you were too weak to hold a book.

I stayed close to you in ICU
and still I didn't hear you ask,
"Am I dying?" I opened the page
to fifty-six, reading until the light
began to fade and it was night.
You slept, so I put down the book.

I moved my chair nearer the bed
to pat your hand or stroke your hair,
swab your mouth, massage your leg.
You'd wanted me to understand
death was already close at hand
and you were finishing your book.

I haven't gone back to chapter
one of the novel you left me
in *medias res*. I feel you must
be in the pages I'm still turning,
turning. See how I'm still learning,
Mother, how to read your book...

Quotidian

She leaves the consolation of her bed,
takes up her trowel, brush or pen
and tames the hours into routine:
more bills to pay, new forms to sign,
the tedious chores, the children to be fed.
A flawless sky, each burning leaf,
indifferent to grief and death,
insists upon this pitiless relief called life:
daily prayer, daily bread, daily risk, daily dread.

Migraine

And a day begins, ordinary
as any other. Ordinary?
What does it mean? Laundry

tumbles in the dryer, the child
is napping, soup is simmering,
weather clement, semblance

of harmony, heaven. Heavenly
light glowing behind everything,
everything has halo, radiance,

tiny sparrows of light darting,
pecking at my eyelids; seconds
later, shipwrecked by nausea,

retching and reeling, blinded
by the terrible ordinary light,
I stumble to bed and ice pack,

praying for anything, praying
deliver me back to boredom,
tedium, begging for the sweet

mercy of argument, tantrum,
breakdown, stasis—anything
but my swollen brain pounding

and pounding and pounding.
Some great thing must come
of this gorgeous shattering;

it must be midwife to something
hard-won and true. Is it wisdom?
Not Wisdom, exigent goddess—

something smaller, something
spent and quiet, blessedly blank
and fragile as glass: is it peace?

Saved Letters

Like a keyhole in the bedroom door—
the rubber band slips off, revealing
foreign postmarks, steamed-off stamps.

> *My darling, I count the minutes ... Did you forget?*

Don't, I think, as the kettle boils for tea.
Let them be. Leave them folded in the past,
in their pale blue airmail world of courtship,

> *How could you ... but when? ... At least she never*

gossip, lies. Don't you believe me? Listen
to them: back in the bureau drawer, forever
locked in cries of love and rage and grief...

> *suffered ... I so wanted ... What did you mean?*

My Memoir
An unauthorized autobiography

Lately, all my friends say, "I am writing my memoir."
The phrase has a certain cachet: in *my* memoir...

... at the precise moment of my birth all the roosters
in Havana crowed in unison, or so I shall say in my memoir.

The thirteenth fairy arrived at my christening with gifts:
beribboned attributes all here on display, in my memoir.

My parents rocked me in a warm cat's cradle of laced arms—
every night, Brahms lulled, I still sway in my memoir.

We played with lightning in my grandfather's big house;
after the accident, there was hell to pay in my memoir.

Later, in college, I avoided conventional humiliations
with an aplomb that bordered on blasé, in my memoir.

Everything I owned could be packed neatly in one suitcase—
from the baby grand down to my negligée, in my memoir.

I starred in my share of intrigues and wild affairs:
Paris, the Seventies. But I don't care for exposé in my memoir.

For a dizzying decade, I pedaled through marriage and career,
credentials that I modestly downplay in my memoir.

Least Wicked Stepmother and Most Promising Perfectionist—
I can't help but mention the two (touché) in my memoir.

My own infanta's birth was graced by doves and portents;
see how she grows taller in every way, in my memoir.

This part is true: I write in my sleep with a fountain pen—
the sheets are streaked with indigo by day, in my memoir.

My house is haunted by a blue-green imago and a ghost whose silver saxophone still plays and plays, in my memoir.

At my funeral, the eulogies to Blake were deeply affecting. People were so bereft I decided to stay, in my memoir...

Proverbs of Hell
William Blake

Drive your cart, and plow over the bones of the dead.

That afternoon she sat, chain-smoking under a broad-
leafed oak until, one by one, the night put out its stars.

At her feet, a cardboard box: harmonica, an open fifth
of scotch, his stamp collection, a medal won during the war.

They'd known each other less and less: this absence
stung no more than salt rubbed in a wound's old scars.

She crumpled the empty pack, carried the box across wet
grass and gravel, and stowed it in the dark trunk of her car.

The road of excess leads to the palace of wisdom.

Leave then. Try anything. Perhaps you'll learn
that on a pyre of greed your heart will burn
with pure infant lust; you will squander your
inheritance, become a cliché and a bore.

But when you sicken of that feast and turn
back to the home that you, Prodigal, spurn
for tavern, brothel, games of chance and more—
your father waits to greet you at the door.

Eternity is in love with the productions of time.

Like any amorist
writing and rewriting
a *blason*, she could list
his physical charms, but

everything about him,
she'll tell you, intrigues her.
The complicated math
of moon and water stirs

her imagination,
the sweet flow of season
into season; planets
in concentric orbits

spinning through the skies
exhilarate her; she's
undone by night's dark eyes,
and languid under noon's

high glare, midnight's quiet
touch, and when dawn beckons,
she aches for dusk, an hour's
stroke, the sweep of second

hands, for calendars, years,
metronomes, the giddy
carillon, the solemn bell.
It all adds up, but he

is helpless, he can't stop
these proofs of industry,
these cataracts of gifts;
she notices each drop,

and loves that he can't quit.
Every day, on her wrist,
another dainty watch.
But if pressed, she'll admit

the new digital ones
displease her. She so loves
the heartbeat of a clock:
the *tick*—the pause—the *tock*.

No bird soars too high, if he soars on his own wings.

But in every generation, it seems, they try,
remembering not the fall, but the heady
lift of flight, the eagle soaring by.
Like wax-winged Icarus, all too ready
to borrow shiny wings and gain the sky,
they risk the fearful plummet to earth or sea
and stunned like garden birds who cannot see
the plate glass air of windows, unsteady,
numb with yearning, they rise again to fly.

A Book of Hours

The pigeons hovering on the windowsill
insist on mating noisily until
   they climax and I wake to their aubade
of protests and goodbyes against their will.

Night cedes the way and dawn begins to seep
between the blinds and into morning sleep,
   but I resist the overture to rise.
There is a dream I'm trying hard to keep.

Two lovers in a king-size bed, and one
is reaching for the other, who has gone
   and left her, lonely as Penelope.
Why is it that the birds all sing at dawn?

I picture you out jogging in the park,
each step advancing through receding dark
   while I hove further into last night's dream
of harmony between the owl and lark.

The starving garbage trucks are breaking fast.
They feed on leftovers not meant to last
   and clear the streets of what's put out at night:
the cat, torn clothes, a cigarette, the past.

My day begins in earnest when I leave,
appointments humming in a busy heave
   of schedules, notes and lists: mnemonic tricks
I tuck into a neat blue pin-striped sleeve.

At noon I get your voice mail on the phone,
"Please leave a message when you hear the tone,"
   it pleasantly requests, though I suspect
machines have an agenda of their own.

The babysitter calls, she will be late—
the subway stops, the bus stalls or some fate
    prevents her prompt arrival at the school.
Meanwhile, it is the child who has to wait.

But we all wait, and while we wait we learn
that even after marriage we still burn;
    despite the saint all poets love to quote,
there's always something else for which we yearn.

The population pours into the street
at five. I join the eager-to-retreat-
    from-work's-bewildered-world as twilight falls
around, between, beneath the rushing feet.

Above the crowds, striations of the sky
unravel evening and go floating by;
    in tangled skeins of pink and violet
the day's unstrung, the air turns lazuli.

Light yields to the crepuscular embrace
of darkness swiftly filling every space.
    There's nothing lonelier than urban dusk
or lovelier than its solitary grace.

I tried to kill time with a drink or two
in a posh midtown bar, but since I knew
    delaying tactics never beat the clock,
I turned and headed up the avenue.

And thought: not puppets in a box so much
as constellations circling in a clutch
    around the pole; no longer side by side
or face to face, it's head to toe we touch.

The velvet hour of vigils starts to chime,
apartment windows brightly pantomime
    the stars aglow in deep obsidian skies,
each household in its fashion marking time.

You lie in bed, while I stare at a screen
and wait until the ghost in my machine
   awakes and calls the Angel, Duende, Muse—
capricious visitors—to intervene.

"It's after midnight, are you coming soon?"
you ask, emerging from a dream's cocoon,
   confused and plaintive. Yes, I lie, and then
resume my late communion with the moon.

Little Spanish Lessons

One word—*sueño*—serves for sleeping
and dreaming, the twin labors of the night.

And *pluma* stands for both pen and feather—
feather as wing, synecdoche for flight.

The Art of Translation

The family sleeps,
but quietly at her desk the translator
sits among piles of books: dictionaries
in many languages, dead and spoken,
grammars, biographies of all concerned.
Beside her the dog stirs, whimpering
in a dream; the night composes
an adagio of appliances and breath
as she thumbs through pages, making
meticulous notes, an ocean of crumpled
possibilities rising in a white tide at her feet.

Pale in the light
of the computer screen she labors;
although the rules of her trade require
a subtle balance of accuracy and beauty,
she suspects she's after something else.
Tonight, for instance, she has rendered
"Havana, 1961" as *revolution box*;
and just yesterday, "Father" turned
into *jazzman* one night and *soldier*
the next; then "Permanent Address"
seemed best expressed as *house of words*.

How else to speak
of the meaning of home? Somewhere,
somewhere in this legacy of stories
told and retold in a private language
of the heart, the land yields, the harvest
is rich. She's heard it said that memory
has no translation; "We know it well
in a beloved version and we know it too
well in desolation." Still, she keeps
at it, late into the night, mantled in silence,
working and reworking this lexicon magic.

Notes

"Carnation, Lily, Lily, Rose" owes its inspiration and several phrases to a review by Deborah Weisgall, which appeared in *The New York Times* on July 27, 1997.

"American Girl®" is indebted to Elizabeth Bishop's "Cirque d'Hiver" for the form.

The epigraph to section III is taken from a quote by Geoff Dyer in *Out of Sheer Rage*, NorthPoint Press (1999), which itself relies on a quote from the architect Vincenzo Volentieri.

The lines quoted in the concluding stanza of "The Art of Translation" are paraphrased from the poem "From Amherst to Kashmir," section 7, "Memory," by Agha Shahid Ali, and can be found in *Rooms Are Never Finished*, W.W. Norton (2001).

The Richard Snyder Publication Series

This book is the tenth in a series honoring the memory of Richard Snyder (1925-1986), poet, fiction writer, playwright and longtime professor of English at Ashland University. Snyder served for fifteen years as English Department chair, and was co-founder (in 1969) and co-editor of the Ashland Poetry Press, an adjunct of the university. He was also co-founder of the Creative Writing major at the school, one of the first on the undergraduate level in the country. In selecting the manuscript for this book, the editors kept in mind Snyder's tenacious dedication to craftsmanship and thematic integrity.

Snyder Award Winners:
1997: Wendy Battin for *Little Apocalypse*
1998: David Ray for *Demons in the Diner*
1999: Philip Brady for *Weal*
2000: Jan Lee Ande for *Instructions for Walking on Water*
2001: Corrinne Clegg Hales for *Separate Escapes*
2002: Carol Barrett for *Calling in the Bones*
2003: Vern Rutsala for *The Moment's Equation*
2004: Christine Gelineau for *Remorseless Loyalty*
2005: Benjamin S. Grossberg for *Underwater Lengths in a Single Breath*
2006: Lorna Knowles Blake for *Permanent Address*
2007: Helen Wallace for *Shimming the Glass House*